Queensland. Department of Government Stores

Contract Prices for 1900 and 1901

Queensland. Department of Government Stores

Contract Prices for 1900 and 1901

ISBN/EAN: 9783743311817

Manufactured in Europe, USA, Canada, Australia, Japa

Cover: Foto ©ninafisch / pixelio.de

Manufactured and distributed by brebook publishing software
(www.brebook.com)

Queensland. Department of Government Stores

Contract Prices for 1900 and 1901

INDEX TO CONTENTS.

INDEX TO CONTRACTS.

GENERAL CONDITIONS OF GOVERNMENT STORES CONTRACTS.

1. The envelope containing the Tender must be endorsed "*Tender for Supplies, 1900 and 1901.*"

2. The lowest or any tender will not necessarily be accepted.

3. Attached to each Tender there must be a memorandum signed by the party tendering, and two responsible persons as sureties, agreeing to be answerable for the due performance of the contract, in the event of the Tender being accepted, and undertaking, in such case, that they will severally execute and deliver, at the Office of the Government Storekeeper, in Brisbane, within fourteen days from the notification of acceptance of the Tender, a bond to Her Majesty for securing such performance, computed at 10 per centum on the estimated value of the Tender.

4. It will be optional for persons to Tender for any one or more of the classes into which the supplies are divided, but no Tender will be received for only a portion of the articles enumerated in any one class.

5. The Tenders must state the price at which each article tendered for is to be supplied.

6. Customs duties, and the value of all packages, are to be included in the prices named.

7. A sample of such of the articles to be tendered for as are marked in the Schedules with an asterisk may be seen at the Government Stores; where no samples are shown, it is to be understood that the articles shall be the best of their several kinds. The sample may in some respects be approximate, and is to be read in view of the fuller particulars given in the Schedules.

8. It must be distinctly understood that, where special brands of goods or makers' names are used in the Schedules, only goods fulfilling those conditions will be accepted. In other cases, articles equal in every respect to the sealed samples may be supplied.

9. In the case of those Schedules where no quantities are expressed the contractor will be bound to furnish as much or as little of the articles tendered for as may be required. Some of the items may not be required at all. Quantities taken in previous periods can be seen; but it must be understood that no quantities are guaranteed, and the information given is without prejudice.

10. Where weight or measurement is expressed, and the articles tendered fall short of the stipulation, the Government Storekeeper may, should he think fit to accept the articles, make a rateable reduction from the price, calculated proportionately by the value per unit of the expressed weight or measure, or he may accept such portion as fulfil the terms of the contract, and reject the remainder.

11. In the case of articles which, upon examination, *after delivery*, are found defective, the Government Storekeeper may call upon the contractor to replace same with the proper article, and may refuse payment or certificate for payment until due substitution is made.

12. When goods of any one kind are delivered in large quantities they shall be in original packages, but no claim will be allowed for such packages.

13. In cases of urgency the Government Storekeeper may purchase any of the articles enumerated from others than the contractor.

14. In the event of any articles not included in the Schedules being purchased from a contractor, a discount of 2½ per cent. will be deducted on payment for same.

15. In the event of any failure or delay on the part of a contractor in supplying articles as required, they may after forty-eight hours' default be procured by the Government Storekeeper at the risk and expense of the contractor, and the excess of cost, if any, shall be deducted from any moneys payable to the contractor.

16. In the event of a difference of opinion between a contractor and the Government Storekeeper as to the quality of any articles supplied, the decision of the Minister shall be final and binding upon the contractor.

17. It is to be distinctly understood that the conditions of these contracts are not to be considered as infringed by the Government should they obtain similar supplies under other departmental contracts.

18. It shall be in the power of the Government to terminate a contract forthwith on the report of the Government Storekeeper that persistent irregularity exists in the quality of articles tendered, or that unnecessary delay in delivery or in replacing them when required occurs; the defaulting contractor shall, however, retain the privilege of delivering, as required, articles bearing a distinctive Government mark or brand to the extent of the shipments, not exceeding the stipulated quantity, he may then have *en route*.

T. M. KING,

MEMORANDA RELATING TO REQUISITIONS ON THE GOVERNMENT STOREKEEPER

FOR

STATIONERY

AND

OFFICE REQUISITES.

--- ◆ ---

THESE should be made on the Government Storekeeper *on the special form provided*, which can be obtained at the Government Printing Office, for a six or twelve months' supply, according to the extent and work of each office, *care being taken to state on the Requisition the period for which the supply is asked.*

The columns provided for "Last Supply" and "Stock on hand" should be *carefully filled in*, otherwise the Requisition may be returned for amendment.

Applications should be prepared at the *close* of March and [or] September by—

> All Officers in the Departments under the Chief or Home Secretaries,
>
> Gold Wardens and Mineral Land Commissioners,
>
> Land Agents and Land Commissioners;

and at the *close* of June and [or] December by—

> All other Officers and Departments.

The stationery requirements of the Police and Prisons will accompany their annual or semi-annual demands for general Stores.

In accordance with the Executive Minutes of January and July, 1889, articles made in the Government Institutions have to be paid for by the Department asking for them: the price is assessed at the cost of the material only.

By direction of the same minutes, surveyor's and drawing materials are also supplied at the expense of those asking for them.

In preparing their requisitions Public Officers will please note that the enumeration of any particular article in the following schedules does not necessarily warrant application for it as a *free issue*. The majority of lines there appearing are provided for the service of those Departments and Institutions, having maintenance votes, who pay for their requirements on the certificate of the Government Storekeeper.

No. 1.

STATIONERY.

Thomas Brown and Sons, Limited.

Attention is directed to the General Conditions set out in *Gazette* notice.

* Denotes that a sample is shown, but as it may be approximate it is to be read in conjunction with any fuller description given herein.

The quantities named in the margin are those that will be required, and except as otherwise stated, delivery must be made of one-fourth as at the first day of the months of January and July in each year. The Contractor must, however, supply immediately on demand any additional quantities that may be asked for.

Articles.		£	s.	d.
*Baskets—Table, wicker, demy ... ... per doz.		2	2	0
* „ „ wire, 9½ in. x 14 in. ... ... „		1	3	0
* „ Waste paper, 12 in. deep, 17 in. dia. at top „		1	0	0
* „ „ 11 in. „ 14 in. „ „			18	0
*Bibles, ruby, 16mo ... ... „			7	0
*Blotting-pads, 12 in. x 18 in. overall, fitted with black leather corners, and furnished with 24 single sheets of 38 lb. white blotting ... ... „		1	2	0
*Bodkins—Plain ... ... „			4	0
* „ With eye ... ... „			4	3
*Brushes—Damping, Hair, 3½-in. ... ... „			8	0
* „ „ Felt, 4-in. ... ... „			13	0
* „ Gum ... ... „				6
*Cardboard, 6-sheet, foolscap single, 13 in. x 8½ ... per 100			2	2
*Cards—Plain, white, 2½ in. x 3¾ in., 50's ... ... per doz. pkts.			1	9
* „ „ „ 4½ in. x 6 in., 50's ... ... „			7	0
* „ Playing ... ...per doz. packs			4	0
*Clips—Foolscap board, 15 in. x 10 in. ... ... per doz.			10	0
* „ Hand ... ... „			7	3
*Copy presses, 15 in. x 10 in. inside, 100 lb. weight... each		1	5	0
*Copy-press stands, cedar, with drawer ... ... „			13	6
*Cord, silk, green, in skeins ... ... per doz.			3	6
*Date-boxes—Revolving ... ... „		1	2	6
* „ Tin, 8-in. ... ... „		1	4	6
* „ „ 4½-in. ... ... „			8	6
*Drying-sheets, 13½ in. x 9½ in. ... ... per 1,000		1	10	0
*Elastic bands—Variegated, 200 in a box ... per doz. boxes			6	0
* „ „ Perry's Imperial, No. 6, aromatic red, flat, ½-gross boxes ... ... „		4	0	0
* „ „ Flat, assorted, 4 sizes, ½-gross boxes „		1	7	0
* „ „ Round, assorted, Perry's extra strong. No. 6 series, 6 sizes, 5 oz., ½-gross boxes ... ... „		2	5	0
*Ferret, green, ¼-in., in pieces of 36 yards ... per doz. pieces		1	10	0

Articles.		Price.		
		£	s.	d.
*Files—Hook, 9 in., 12 in., and 16 in.	per doz.		2	6
* „ Stab, brass wire, 6 in., 22-oz.	„		11	0
* „ Apron, foolscap	„		8	6
*Gum bottles, cap and brush	„		9	0
*Indiarubber, White	...per doz. pieces		2	10
Ink, Stephens', in Stone—				
oz.				
No. 5, Blue-black Writing, 40	per doz.	1	4	6
No. 10, „ Copying, 40	„	1	4	6
No. 52, Violet-Noire „ 27	„	1	2	6
No. 37, Scarlet ... 12	„		17	0
Violet, Non-copying, 12	„		17	0
* „ Antoine's copying, 30-oz.	„	1	0	0
* „ Rubber Stamp, assorted colours, 1-oz. ...	..		5	0
* „ Metallic „ „ ½-oz. ...	„		11	6
* „ Neo cyclostyle	„	1	6	0
*Ink and Pencil Erasers—A. W. Faber's large ..	„		5	8
* „ „ „ Hardmuth's „ ...	„		5	2
* „ „ „ A. W. Faber's small ...	„		2	10
* „ „ „ Hardmuth's „ ...	„		2	6
* „ extractors	„		3	0
„ pads, everlasting, assorted colours, 6 in. x 3½ in.	„		15	0
* „ „ „ „ 4 in. x 3 in.	„		10	0
*Inkstands—Round, glass, metal fall top	„		7	3
* „ Pewter, cap, 4-in. base	„		18	0
* „ „ cap, and 7-in. plate	„	1	6	0
* „ Square, cut-glass, with glass loose lids, 14oz.	„		15	6
* „ Walnut, 3-well	„	1	16	0
* „ Oak „	„	1	16	0
*Ink-wells, porcelain, No. 3, 4, and 5	„			9
„ glass „ „	„			9
*Knives, desk	„		12	0
* „ erasing	„		7	0
*Labels, buckram, with eye, 5½ in. x 2¾ in.	per 1,000		8	0
* „ cartridge, with eye, 5½ in. x 2¾ in.	„		2	6
* „ „ „ 4 in. x 1½ in.	„		2	6
*Laces, green silk, 36 in.	per gross	1	14	0
*Letter Balances, 16-oz.	each		7	6
* „ 8-oz.	„		5	3
* „ Salter's 16-oz.	per doz.	1	8	0
*Memorandum books, pocket, large, ruled	„		9	0
* „ „ „ small „	„		7	0
* „ „ Penny's metallic, large ...	„	1	10	0
* „ „ „ small ...	„	1	4	0
„ „ Penny's insides, large	„		9	3
„ „ „ small	„		6	3
„ ., 8vo., 36 leaves, ruled	„			8
„ „ „ „ „ and single money	„			8
*Millboards, marbled, 9 x 14¾, 14 oz.	per 100	1	2	0
* „ „ „ 9 oz.	„		16	0

STATIONERY—*continued.*

Articles.		Price.		
		£	s.	d.
PAPER—				
* Copying, foolscap single, 5-quire divisions ...	per ream		1	9
Cyclostyle, Gestetner's, duplicating	per quire		3	0
* Oiled royal, hand-made (480 sheets)	per ream	3	10	0
*Paper binders, Premier, 1 gross in box, 631	per doz. boxes		6	0
* ,, ,, ,, ,, ,, 632 ...	,,		7	9
* ,, ,, ,, ,, ,, 643 ...	,,		13	0
* ,, ,, ,, ,, ,, 644 ...	,,		15	6
* ,, ,, ,, ,, ,, 645 ...	,,		19	0
* ,, ,, brass, round head, Premier, No. 0 or Micros	,,		3	9
* ,, ,, brass, round head, Premier, ½-gross in box, assorted, 741, 742, 743, 6d. boxes	,,		3	3
,, ,, McGill's staples, No. 1, 200 in box	per 1,000		3	9
,, ,, ,, No. 2, ,,	,,		5	0
*Paper knives, stout ivory, 10-in.	per doz.	1	4	9
* ,, ,, steel ,, ...	,,		5	9
* ,, weights, *lead*, covered throughout with stout purple basil, 4 lb. each	,,	1	1	6
* ,, weights, *lead*, baize-lined, 1¼ lb. each ...	,,		8	6
* ,, ,, glass, 14 oz.	,,		14	6
*Paste—Stickphasts, 1s. bottles, cap and brush ...	,,		9	3
* ,, Gloy ,, ,, ...	,,		8	6
PENCILS—				
* Drawing, hexagon, A.W. Faber, any No. or letter	per gross	1	4	0
* ,, ,, Koh-i-noor, any degree ...	,,	2	0	6
* Black office, assorted letters	,,		6	6
* Blue, best quality	,,		18	6
* ,, ,, thick	,,		16	0
* Green ,, ...	,,		18	6
* Red ,, ...	,,	1	2	0
* Red and blue combined, best quality	,,	1	11	6
* Eagle automatic, 872 green	per doz.		9	0
* ,, ,, 5-inch black, stop gauge ...	,,		7	0
* ,, ,, 3¼-inch black ,, ...	,,		7	0
Leads—				
For Eagle automatic pencils—				
For 872 green	...per doz. leads		1	8
3½-inch copying, No. 3	,,			10
*Pen-cleaners, hair, with shields	per doz.		12	0
PENHOLDERS—				
* Long, cedar	per gross		3	3
* Short ,, ...	,,		3	0
* Cane, thick, Johann Faber	,,		12	0
* Eagle	,,		15	0
* Lytton	,,	2	14	0
*Pen-racks	per doz.		7	6

STATIONERY—*continued.*

Articles.				Price.		
				£	s.	d.

PENS—

  Barrel (12 in a box)—

Mitchell's 4/L, 60/M, 350/N, 36/0257	...per doz. boxes		4	0	
„ S	„		5	9	
Gillott's 225, 8/F, 8/M, and 2/B	„		11	6	

  Nibs—

Mitchell's 2/G, 50/J, and 2/R, 1 gross in a box,	„		18	0
Mitchell's gilt J, ¼-gross in box	„		13	6
Gillott's 19/292, 45/293, 28/294, 24/404, and 4/729, 1 gross in a box	„		13	6
Gillott's 3/170 and 1/353, 1 gross in a box ...	„		18	9
„ 2/303 and 2/387 „ „ ...	„	1	16	0
Brandauer's 6d. boxes, any number	„		3	9
McNiven and Cameron, 1s. boxes, any name	„		6	9
Hewitt's ball-pointed, 1s. boxes, any name or number	„		8	0
* Mitchell's red ink, 12 on a card ...	...per doz. cards		7	0
* *Lithographic,* crow-quill, 659, 12 on a card ...	per card		1	0
* *Perryian,* 6 on a card	„		1	6
* *Quill, best,* in packets of 25	per 1,000	1 1	1	0
*Post and delivery cages	per doz.	1	4	0
*Pounce, 1 oz. packets, Morell's	per gross of pkts.	1 7		0
*Rulers, ebony, round—12-inch, 7½ oz.	per doz.		8	9
* „ „ „ 18 „ 14½ „	„	1	0	0
* „ „ „ 24 „ 19 „	„	1	10	0
*Seals, Red, adhesive (legal seal). ½ in.. 72 in box, per gross of bxs.			18	0
* „ „ „ (vandyked), 2⅜ in.	per 1,000		10	0
*Scissors—8 in.	per doz.		15	0
* „ 6 „	„		8	9
*Sponge bowls, glass, 3½ in., with ¼-oz. *Turkey* sponges	„		8	9
*Stationery racks	„	3	0	0
*Tape, red, linen, 9 yards in a piece, No. 32 ...	per gross of 144 pieces		13	0
* „ „ „ „ No. 24	„		9	6
* „ „ „ „ No. 16	„		7	9
*Water-wells, 4½ in. slit	per doz.		12	0
*Wax—Hard India, in boxes, 20 to the lb. ...	per lb.		3	10
* „ Express „ 10 to the lb.	„	1	1½	
* „ Fine „ 8 „	„		3¼	

STATIONERY—*continued.*

The following are also in Stock at the Government Stores:—

Almanacks—Pugh's.
Arm or Ledger Rests.
Books—
  Deposition, " Medium," in 250's and 500's.
  Demy, faint ruled, 2, 3, 4, and 6 quire.
  Foolscap, faint ruled, 2, 3, and 4 quire.
      „   „   single and double money, 2, 3, and 4 quire.
  Guard, skeleton or interleaved, both in foolscap and demy.
  Judge's Note.
  Letter-press Copy, 250's 500's, and 1,000's.
  Memo forms, printed and numbered, bound in 100's.
Boxes and Holders for Toilet Paper.
Chalk Sticks.
Clips, corner, brass, in boxes of 100.
Diaries—Wood's Australian, in pocket, 8vo, 4to, and foolscap.
Files, Newspaper.
Gazette covers, pairs.
Ink—
  Stephens' Penny Bottles—Black and red.
  Watson, Ferguson, and Co.'s—Blue-black and scarlet.
Mackintosh copying sheets, foolscap, single.
Oil sheets, foolscap single, for press copying.
Paper, toilet.
Pens, fountain—" Swan," " Marvel," and " Independent."
Pencils—
  Copying, in wood.
  Black parcel.
Pencil-sharpeners
Rubber Stamps, O.H.M.S.
Rubber Stamping Blocks, ¾ in., 12 in. x 12 in.
Scribbling blocks.
Staples for " Star" machines.
Staple presses, " Star" automatic.
      „   McGill's, No. 1.
Typewriters.
Typewriting Carbons and Ribbons.

No. 2.

ENVELOPES.

Webster and Co.

Attention is directed to the General Conditions set out in *Gazette* notice.

* Denotes that a sample is shown, but as it may be approximate it is to be read in conjunction with any fuller description given herein.

The quantities named in the margin are those that will be required, and except as otherwise stated, delivery must be made of one-fourth as at the first day of the months of January and July in each year. The Contractor must, however, supply immediately on demand any additional quantities that may be asked for.

In view of the foregoing provision, the Government Storekeeper will, in the event of a Contractor not becoming a successful tenderer, upon the next following occasion of calling for supplies, relieve him of any reasonable quantity of such of the within-named Envelopes as bear a distinctive Government mark.

The weights when named are exclusive of wrappers.

Articles.		Price. £	s.	d.
*Cloth lined, cream, all cameoed—				
Special, pocket shape, 14¼ in. x 9½ in.	per 1,000	7	2	6
Long „ „ 16 in. x 6 in.	„	5	2	6
Large, high flaps, 12 in. x 6 in. ...	„	5	4	0
*Cartridge, all cameoed—				
Extra large, pocket shape, 16 in. x 10½ in. ...	„	2	8	0
Special „ „ 14¼ in. x 9½ in. ...	„	1	18	6
Long „ „ 16 in. x 6 in. ...	„	1	6	6
Foolscap, high flaps, 9 in. x 4½ in.	„	0	15	3
Linen, decoratively boxed, plain flaps—				
* Parchment, in 100's—				
5¼ in. x 4¼ in., 12½ lb.	„	1	9	0
4¾ in. x 3¾ in., 10 lb.	„	1	1	0
* Vellum, in 100's –				
5¼ in. x 4¼ in., 10¼ lb.	„		13	7
4¾ in. x 3¾ in., 8¼ lb.	„		10	5
*Antique vellum, plain, packeted in 250's—				
5¼ in. x 4¼ in., 8¾lb.	„		5	4
4¾ in. x 3¾ in., 7lb.	„		3	7
*Cream, all cameoed, except one—				
Long, pocket shape, 16 in. x 6 in.	„	1	0	10
Large, high flaps, 12 in. x 6 in.	„	1	1	7
Demy, „ 11 in. x 5 in.	„		14	5
Foolscap, high flaps, 9 in. x 4 in., 12 lb. ...	„		6	9
„ pocket shape, 9 in. x 4 in., 12 lb. ...	„		8	4
Letter, common flaps, 5½ in. x 3⅛ in., 6 lb. ...	„		4	0
„ „ „ 5½ in. x 3⅛ in., 6 lb., not cameoed	„		3	6
Note, „ 4¾ in. x 2¾ in., 4½ lb. ...	„		3	6

ENVELOPES—*continued.*

Articles.				Price. £ s. d.
*Blue, all cameoed—				
Long, pocket shape, 16 in. x 6 in.	...	...	per 1,000	1 3 3
Large, high flaps, 12 in. x 6 in. ...	...	...	,,	1 5 7
Demy, ,, 11 in. x 5 in. ...	...	...	,,	15 3
Letter, common flaps, 5½ in. x 3¼ in., 6 lb.	...	...	..	4 2
Buff, all printed cameoes and O H.M.S.—				
* Foolscap, high flaps, 9 in. x 4 in., 7 lb. ...	..	,,		5 3
* ,, packet post, pocket shape, flap not gummed, 9 in. x 4 in., 7 lb. ...	...	..		4 10
* Letter, high flaps, 5½ in. x 3½ in., 3½ lb.	...	,,		2 5
* Special, pockets, 10½ in. x 6¾ in., 12 lb.	...	,,		7 6
Stone, printed cameo, and O.H.M.S.—				
* Special, high flaps, 5½ in. x 4 in., 10 lb.		,,		5 10

The following lines of Envelopes are also in Stock at Government Stores :—

Cloth lined, cream, cameoed, pocket-shape—
15½ in. x 11 in. ; 16 in. x 10½ in. ; and 18 in. x 12 in.
Cartridge, cameoed :—
11 in. x 5 in. ; 12 in. x 6 in. ; and 18 in. x 12 in.
Linen, bank, high flaps —
Letter, plain, 5½ in. x 3¼ in.
Cream—
Foolscap, plain, common flaps, 9 in. x 4 in.
Blue —
Foolscap, cameo, common flaps, 9 in. x 4 in.
Buff —
Special, 9¾ in. x 6½ in.
Duplex : azure outside, blue in—
Letter, plain, 5¼ in. x 4½ in.

No. 3.

PAPER.

Webster and Co.

Attention is directed to the General Conditions set out in *Gazette* notice.

* Denotes that a sample is shown, but as it may be approximate it is to be read in conjunction with any fuller description given herein.

The quantities named in the margin are those that will be required, and, unless otherwise stated, delivery must be made of one-fourth as at the first day of the months of January and July in each year. The Contractor must, however, supply immediately on demand any additional quantities that may be asked for.

The expressed weight of all papers is net, and exclusive of wrappers.

All folded writing papers to be supplied with cut edges.

Writing, cartridge, blotting, and brown papers to contain 480 *good* sheets to the ream, and to be folded, except as otherwise expressed.

Litho. papers to be supplied flat and without water-mark, and to contain 500 good sheets to the ream.

Articles.		Price.		
		£	s.	d.
Linen—				
Foolscap, Double—				
* Bank, 14 lb., flat ...	per ream		8	11
* Extra strong, 30 lb., flat	,,		17	3
Foolscap—				
* O.T.M., 20 lb., flat, cut edges	,,	1	2	9
* Extra strong, 14 lb., folded	,,		9	0
* ,, 14 ,, ,, and ruled ...	,,		9	5
* ,, 14 ,, flat, ruled, double money, head and ref. lines both sides ...	,,		11	3
* Bank, single sheets, cut edges, 3½ lb ...	,,		2	6
Large Post 4to—				
* Extra strong, 8½ lb., folded and ruled to pattern	,,		7	3
* Extra strong, 4½ lbs. single and ruled to pattern, cut edges	,,		3	8
Large Post 8vo. decoratively boxed—				
* Bank, 38 oz., in 5 quires	,,		3	1
* Parchment, 8 lb., in 2½ quires, 3-sheet folds	,,		12	0
* Vellum, 7 lb., in 5 quires, 6-sheet folds	,,		7	2
Small Post 8vo. decoratively boxed—				
* Parchment, 6½ lb., in 2½ quires, 3-sheet folds	,,		10	0
* Vellum, 5½ lb., in 5 quires, 6-sheet folds	,,		5	10
Cream—				
Large post, flat, plain, 24 lb., cut edges	,,		7	7
,, folded and ruled, 24 lb.	,,		8	11
Foolscap, double, flat, 30 lb.	,,		9	11
,, folded, 14 lb.	,,		5	4
,, ,, and ruled, 14 lb.	,,		5	9
,, single sheets, 7 lb., cut edges	,,		2	8

PAPER—*continued.*

Articles.		Price. £ s. d

Cream—continued :

Large post 4to, folded, 8½ lb.	per ream	3 5
„ „ „ and ruled, 8½ lb.	„	3 10
„ 8vo. „ 4¼ lb.	„	1 10
„ „ „ and ruled, 4¼ lb. ...	„	2 0

Azure, all folded and ruled—

Large post, 24 lb. ...	„	8 7
Foolscap, 14 lb. ...	„	5 2
Large post, 4to, 12 lb.	„	4 5
„ 8vo, 6 lb.	„	2 3

Litho. Printing—

Demy, double, 40 lb.	„	10 0
„ „ 54 „	„	13 6
„ „ 72 „	„	18 0
Imperial, 45 lb.	„	11 3
„ 55 lb.	„	13 9
Elephant, double, 75 lb.	„	18 9
„ „ 120 lb.	„	1 10 0

Brown (all folded)—

Imperial, rough, 60 lb.	„	6 8
„ double, rough, 120 lb.	„	13 4
„ Ochre glazed, 60 lb.	„	7 9
„ „ 120 lb.	„	15 6

Blotting (demy, folded, packed in ½ reams)—

White, 38 lb.	„	15 6
Pink, 38 lb.	„	15 6
White, 28 lb.	„	11 9
Pink, 28 lb.	„	11 9

The following lines of Paper are also in stock at Government Stores :—

Cartridge—
Imperial, flat, both rough and smooth.
Linen—
Brief, foolscap, flat, hand made.
Litho Printing—
Royal Double, 66 lb.
Foolscap Double, 24 lb
Brown—
Double Imperial, toughened 120 lb.

No. 4.

DRAPERY.

Thomas Brown and Sons, Limited.

Attention is directed to the General conditions set out in *Gazette* notice.

* Denotes that a sample is shown, but as it may be approximate it is to be read in conjunction with any fuller description given herein.

The number of Ordnance Rugs required is 900 annually. A good supply must be always on hand to meet demands.

Articles.		Price. £	s.	d.
*Blankets—Blue, 5ft. 4 in. x 6ft. 9in. each, 6½ lb. a pair	per pair		9	3
* ,, White ,, ,, 7½ lb. ,,	,,		9	5
*Braces, men's cotton	per doz. pairs		5	6
*Braid—Black llama, 1-in.	per gross yds.		5	9
* ,, Double London, 1-in., 2-cord, 2½ lb. to the gross	,,		7	6
* ,, Flannel binding, ⅞-in. (6d.)	,,		6	0
* ,, Scarlet, tubular, ⅝-in.	,,		3	0
* ,, White, Hercules, ⅝-in.	,,		5	6
*Buckles, vest, black or white	per gross			6
*Buckram, black, 30-in.	per yard			3¼
*Bunting, 24-in., any colour ; blue to be true indigo dye	,,			7
*Buttons—Bone, coat, assorted, dark colours	per gross		2	6
* ,, Vegetable ivory	,,		2	6
* ,, China, shirt	,,			1
* ,, For great coats, black	,,		2	6
* ,, Linen, plain, 24 to 28	,,			6
* ,, ,, eyeletted, 24 to 28	,,			9
* ,, Metal bar, trousers, black or white ...	,,			3
* ,, ,, ,, fly ,, ,, ...	,,			2½
* ,, ,, ring, trousers ,, ,, ...	,,			4½
* ,, ,, ,, fly ,, ,, ...	,,			4
* ,, Navy blue compo. dress	,,		1	3
* ,, Smoke pearl	,,		3	3
* ,, White ,, ...	,,		3	1
* ,, V.R. gilt, small	,,		7	0
*Calico—100-inch, bleached, 13½-oz.	per yard		1	5½
* ,, 36-in. ,, 3¼ ,, ...	,,			3⅛
*Collar check, 40-in., 18-oz.	,,		1	5
*Cloth—Scarlet, 60-in.	,,		8	9
* ,, Blue saddle, 54-in., 28-oz., true indigo dye ...	,,		3	1
* ,, Italian, 54-in.	,,		1	6
*Combs—Dressing, 7-in., horn	per doz.		1	7
* ,, Tooth, small, white horn	,,		2	2
*Crash, Russia, 15-in.	per yard			3¾
*Cotton, reels of white or black, Clark's Anchor ...	per gross		14	0
*Damask, unbleached, 66-in.	per yard		1	2¾

DRAPERY—*continued.*

Articles.		Price. £	s.	d.
*Drill—Linen, white, 27-in., $5\frac{1}{2}$-oz.	per yard		1	2
* ,, ,, brown, 27-in., 6-oz.	,,			$8\frac{3}{4}$
*Duck, four bear, 27-in.	,,			$6\frac{7}{8}$
*Dusters—Blue check, 3-oz.	per doz.		3	1
* ,, Feather, China	,,		3	11
* ,, ,, Turkey, No. 12	,,		13	0
*Flannel—29-in., 6-oz.	per yard			10
* ,, House, 24-in.	,,			$5\frac{5}{8}$
*Frieze, 54-in., 27-oz.	,,		3	9
*Forfar, 38-in.	,,			$5\frac{1}{4}$
*Galatea, 29-in.	,,			$5\frac{1}{4}$
*Glass cloths	per doz.		3	10
*Half-hose—Men's, unbleached cotton	per doz. pairs		4	0
* ,, ,, worsted, 4-oz.	,,		10	6
*Hose—Women's, unbleached cotton	,,		5	8
* ,, ,, worsted, 4-oz.	,,		10	8
*Handkerchiefs, pocket, coloured	per doz.		2	8
*Hessian, 72-in., 18-oz.	per yard			$5\frac{1}{2}$
*Holland—Brown, 30-in.	,,			$5\frac{3}{8}$
* ,, Boiled, 33-in	,,			$6\frac{1}{4}$
* ,, Dressed, 34-in.	,,			$5\frac{3}{4}$
* ,, Green window, 36 to 42 in.	,,			7
*Homespun, dark-grey, 29-in., $4\frac{1}{2}$-oz.	,,			$7\frac{3}{4}$
* ,, light-grey, 29-in., $4\frac{1}{2}$-oz.	,,			$7\frac{3}{4}$
*Hooks, waist belt, black	per gross		2	9
*Hooks and eyes—Black or white, 6 to 8	,,			3
* ,, ,, Cloak, black	,,			6
*Huckaback towelling, 27-in., 8-oz.	per yard			$6\frac{3}{4}$
*Laces—Boot, with tag, 44-in.	per gross of pairs		2	4
* ,, ,, kangaroo, 24-in.	,,		4	11
*Leather, black American, 50-in.	per yard		1	4
*Linen, apron, 40-in., $7\frac{1}{2}$ oz.	,,			$7\frac{1}{2}$
*Matting Coir—36-in.	,,		1	9
* ,, 45-in.	,,		2	2
* ,, 54-in.	,,		2	8
*Mops, thrumb	per doz.		11	9
*Moleskin, *undressed*, 30-in., 12-oz.	per yard		1	$0\frac{3}{4}$
*Mosquito net, 90-inch	,,			$6\frac{3}{4}$
Needles, sewing, assorted	per 1,000		1	11
*Night-caps—Men's cotton, white	per doz.		4	6
* ,, ,, worsted, red	,,		9	0
*Print, undressed, assorted, fast colours, 31-in., 3-oz.	per yard			$3\frac{3}{4}$
*Pins—Short whites, 1-oz. packets	per lb.		1	2
* ,, Lill's, 1-oz. packets	,,		2	3
*Pocketing, 29-in.	per yard			$4\frac{1}{2}$
*Quilts, Alhambra, 5 ft. x 7 ft., 4 lb.	each		2	6
Ribbon—Silk, green or blue, in rolls of 36 yards—				
* $\frac{1}{4}$-in.	per doz. pieces		15	0
* $\frac{1}{2}$-in.	,,	1	1	6
* $\frac{3}{4}$-in.	,,	1	12	0

DRAPERY—*continued.*

Articles.		£	s.	d.
*Rugs, Ordnance, red and yellow, 4 ft. 6 in. x 7 ft. 6 in., 3 lb. 9-oz. ...	each		4	$7\frac{1}{2}$
*Serge—Brown, 31-in., $8\frac{1}{2}$-oz. ...	per yard		1	2
* „ Blue, union, 27-in., 8-oz. ...	„			$8\frac{1}{2}$
* „ Navy blue, dress, 44-in. ...	„		1	$8\frac{1}{2}$
* „ White, saddlers', 40-in., 12-oz. ...	„		1	$6\frac{1}{2}$
*Shirting—Scotch twill, *undressed*, 29-in., 5-oz. ...	„			$4\frac{7}{8}$
* „ Indian, 29-in. ...	„			$5\frac{3}{4}$
*Shirts, Scotch twill, contract cloth, any sizes ...	per doz.		17	6
* „ Harvard, fancy, any sizes ...	„	1	4	0
*Sheeting, waterproof, 72-in. ...	per yard		5	9
*Sheets, waterproof, 36 in. x 78 in. ...	each		5	9
*Silesia—Black, 38-in. ...	per yard			5
* „ Slate, 40-in. ...	„			$5\frac{1}{8}$
* „ Striped, 40-in. ...	„			$5\frac{1}{8}$
*Silk—Machine, blk. or scarlet, 1-oz. reels, any number	per lb.	1	0	0
* „ Button-hole twist ...	„	1	0	0
* „ Raven sewings ...	„	1	2	6
*Tape—Black, cotton, $\frac{1}{2}$-in. ...	per gross yds.		1	4
* „ Blocked, India, Nos. 5, 6, or 7 ...	„		2	0
* „ „ „ „ 8, 9, or 10 ...	„		3	0
*Thimbles—Tailors' steel, assorted sizes ...	per doz.			6
* „ Women's „ „ ...	„			$4\frac{1}{2}$
*Thread—Knox's machine, 2-oz. reels, 3-cord, any colour or number ...	per lb.		5	9
* „ Knox's black or white, in hanks ...	„		2	10
*Ticking, bed, linen, 29-in., $10\frac{1}{2}$-oz. ...	per yard			$7\frac{1}{2}$
*Ticklenberg, 27-in., $8\frac{3}{4}$-oz. ...	„			$6\frac{3}{4}$
*Towels—Huckaback, 1 yard contract cloth, hemmed, 8-oz. ...	per doz.		6	9
* „ Turkish, bleached, 8-oz. ...	„		9	9
* „ Bath, $14\frac{3}{4}$-oz. ...	„		19	6
* „ Small hand, $4\frac{1}{4}$-oz. ...	„		5	6
*Trousers, moleskin, contract cloth, any sizes ...	„	2	2	0
*Tweed, all wool, waterproof, true indigo blue, 54-inch	per yard		5	0
*Woollen plaid, 27-in., 4-oz. ...	„			$9\frac{1}{2}$

DRAPERY—*continued.*

The following are in Stock at Government Stores :—

Aprons, linen, for women prisoners.
Armlets—Police Duty badges.
Badges. prisoners', A, B, and C.
Boots, men's and boys' bluchers.
  „   girls' and women's laceups.
Capes, waterproof, for Prison Warders.
Caps, linen, for women prisoners.
Coats, ticklenberg.
  „   over, for Police, Warders. and Watchmen.
  „   tweed, D.B.
Dresses, Scotch twill and brown serge. for women prisoners.
Jackets, frieze, for men prisoners.
  „   Scotch twill and brown serge, for women prisoners.
Jumpers. serge. for Native Police and Water Police.
  „   drill, for Water Police.
Leggings, black leather, 9 x 16, for Police.
  „   brown leather, 7½ x 15.
Nightgowns, unbleached calico.
Petticoats, brown serge and Scotch twill.
Shifts, calico (unbleached) and Scotch twill.
Shirts, flannel and Scotch twill.
Slippers, moleskin.
Trousers. moleskin and tweed.
  „   blue cloth. for Water Police and Native Police
  „   duck. for Water Police and Native Police.
Vests, tweed

No. 5.

BLANKETS.

(Q ⋏ G)

Thomas Brown and Sons, Limited.

Attention is directed to the General Conditions set out in *Gazette* notice.

* Denotes that a sample is shown, but as it may be approximate it is to be read in conjunction with any fuller description given herein.

The blankets are to be similar in colour and quality to sample shown, but of the weight and dimensions named herein, and to be delivered, as required, in original bales of 50 pairs each, packed in tarpaulin, paper, and canvas covers, and dumped so as not to exceed 18 feet cube. The quantity required in the two years is 20,000 pairs, and there must be available each year, if required, 3,000 by 10th January, 3,000 by 10th February, 2,000 by 10th March, and the remainder at any time during the year, as they may be called for.

The border to consist of 3 bands of colour, commencing 6 inches from either end : the centre one being of bright blue, 1 inch wide. Those on either side to be ½-inch wide ; in the case of 16,000 pairs, of bright yellow and of bright red in the remaining 4,000 pairs.

The emblem Q ⋏ G, in letters of about 1 inch in thickness and about 10 inches in length, of bright blue colour, to be wrought in the centre of each pair, in such a way as to render the extraction a matter of difficulty. The fabric to be *afterwards* teased.

Articles.	Price.
	£ s. d.
*Blankets—Grey Q ⋏ G, 4 ft. 6 in. x 6 ft. 6 in. each, 6 lb. per pair ... ... per pair	10 4½

No. 6.

CALICO (UNBLEACHED).

Thomas Brown and Sons, Limited.

Attention is directed to the General Conditions set out in *Gazette* notice. These Calicoes must run the expressed weight of pure Cotton.

Articles.							Price. £ s. d.
*Grey, *undressed*—No. 1, 36-inch,	6 oz.	...	...	per yard			$3\frac{7}{8}$
„ „ „ 72 „	12 „	...		„			$8\frac{7}{8}$
* „ „ No. 2, 36 „	5 „	...	...	„			$3\frac{1}{2}$
„ „ „ 72 „	10 „	...		„			$7\frac{1}{4}$

No. 7.

CLOTH.

Thomas Brown and Sons, Limited.

Attention is directed to the General Conditions set out in *Gazette* notice.

* Denotes that a sample is shown, but as it may be approximate it is to be read in conjunction with any fuller description given herein.

The blue cloths must pass the test for true indigo dye.

The width is to be 54 inches within the listing.

In accordance with the usage of the cloth trade, 37 inches will be required to the yard in length.

Successive supplies of the blue cloths must be of the same shade.

Articles.			Price.		
			£	s.	d.
*Tweed, all wool, small dark patterns, 24 oz.	...	per yard		4	3
*Venetian, all wool, indigo blue, 24 ,,		,,		6	9
*Worsted serge, all wool, indigo blue, 14 ,,		,,		3	9
*Woollen twill, all wool, indigo blue 18 ,,		,,		4	8

No. 8.

HATS AND RIBBONS.

Thomas Brown and Sons, Limited.

Attention is directed to the General Conditions set out in *Gazette* notice.

* Denotes that a sample is shown, but as it may be approximate it is to be read in conjunction with any fuller description given herein.

Hats to be supplied to sizes required.

The quantity of Ribbons required annually are as follows :—" Lucinda" 12, "Otter" 12, "Miner" 6, Water Police 40, H. M. Customs 30.

Articles.		Price.		
			£	s.	d.
*Hats—Women's straw, calico-lined	per doz.		9	6
* ,, Boys' felt, assorted colours and sizes	,,		15	0
* ,, Men's felt, No. 1. assorted colours and sizes	,,	1	2	6
* ,, ,, No. 2, light brown, sizes as required	,,	2	0	0
* ,, Panama, lined and ribbon	,,	3	5	0
Hat ribbons—Q.G.S. "Otter"	,,		6	9
,, ,, ,, " Miner"	,,		6	9
,, ,, ,, " Lucinda"	,,		6	9
,, ,, Water police ...	,,		6	9
,, ,, H. M. Customs... ,,	,,		6	9

No. 9.

HELMETS AND CAPS.

B. Mountcastle and Sons.

Attention is directed to the General Conditions set out in *Gazette* notice.

* Denotes that a sample is shown, but as it may be approximate it is to be read in conjunction with any fuller description given herein.

Helmets and Caps to be supplied to sizes required.

There must not be any Cardboard in the Helmets.

Blue Caps must all pass the test for true indigo dye.

Articles.		Price. £ s. d.
*Helmets, linen drill on gossamer body	each	4 9
*Caps—Prison Warders', pure indigo blue dyed cloth, 1 glazed and 2 white covers each	,,	4 6
* ,, Native Police, pure indigo blue dyed cloth, 1 glazed and 2 white covers each ...	,,	3 0
* ,, Navy, pure indigo blue dyed cloth	,,	1 10

BEDDING.

John Hicks.

Attention is directed to the General Conditions set out in *Gazette* notice.

* Denotes that a sample is shown for style in the case of Mattress Covers and Cases, also Pillow Slips. In respect of the other lines the * indicates that a sample is shown for the cloth to be used.

Articles.		Price.		
		£	s.	d.
Mattresses—				
* Forfar—				
Hay, 2 ft. 6 in. x 6 ft. 3 in. x 4 in. ...	each		4	9
„ 3 ft. x 6 ft. 3 in. x 4 in.... ...	„		5	3
* Linen Tick—				
Fibre, 2 ft. 6 in. x 6 ft. 3 in. x 4 in., 16 lb. ...	„		7	3
„ 3 ft. x 6 ft. 3 in. x 4 in., 22 lb. ...	„		8	3
Kapok, 2 ft. 6 in. x 6 ft. 3 in. x 4 in., 12 lb....	„		13	0
„ 3 ft. x 6 ft. 3 in. x 4 in., 16 lb. ...	„		17	0
*Mattress Cases—				
* Forfar, 2 ft. 6 in. x 6 ft. 3 in. x 4 in.	„		3	0
* „ 3 ft. x 6 ft. 3 in. x 4 in.	„		3	4
*Mattress Covers—				
* Unbleached Calico, 2 ft. 9 in. x 6 ft. 6 in. x 5 in.	„		2	9
* „ „. 3 ft. 3 in. x 6 ft. 6 in. x 5 in.	„		3	0
Pillows—				
* Forfar, hay, 1 ft. 6 in. x 2 ft. 6 in. ...	per doz.		9	0
* Linen Ticking—				
Fibre, 1 ft. 6 in. x 2 ft. 6 in.	„		13	0
Kapok, 1 ft. 6 in. x 2 ft. 6 in.... ...	„		18	6
Pillow Cases—				
* Linen Ticking, 1 ft. 6 in. x 2 ft. 6 in.	„		8	6
* Forfar. 1 ft. 6 in. x 2 ft. 6 in.	„		8	6
*Pillow slips, *white twill calico, 1 ft. 8 in. x 2 ft. 8 in.	„		6	0
Sheets, *unbleached calico, undressed, 12 oz. to the yard, 6 ft. x 7 ft. 6 in.	per pair		3	9

No. 11.

CROCKERY AND TUMBLERS.

Foster and Foster.

Attention is directed to the General Conditions set out in *Gazette* notice.

* Denotes that a sample is shown, but as it may be approximate it is to be read n conjunction with any fuller description given herein.

Tumblers to have Q.G. encircled by a ribbon engraved on the side.

Articles.			Price. £ s. d.
*White Granite Cups and Saucers, squat	...	per doz.	4 3
* ,, Plates, 11-in. overall		,,	4 0
* ,, Bowls, 6-in. overall	...	,,	4 0
*Tumblers, cut, 10¾-oz. ...		,,	9 6

There are also in Stock at the Government Stores—

Earthenware Water-bottles, size 2. about 2 quarts.

No. 12.

BRUSHWARE.

Perry Brothers.

Attention is directed to the General Conditions set out in *Gazette* notice.
* Denotes that a sample is shown, but as it may be approximate it is to be read in conjunction with any fuller description given herein.

Articles.		Price.		
		£	s.	d.
*Brooms—Bass	... ... per doz.		15	0
* ,, Millet, 16-in., 4 tie	... ... ,,		15	0
* ,, Hair	... ... ,,	1	14	0
* ,, Turk's head ...	... ... each		2	6
* . ,, Flat deck	... ... ,,		1	3
*Brushes—Scrubbing	... ... per doz.		7	0
* ,, Whitewash, 3-knot, 8-oz.	... ,,	2	16	0
* ,, Paint, copper-bound, grey middles, Kent's—				
4·0's	... ... each		3	9
6·0's	... ... ,,		4	3
8·0's	... ... ,,		5	6
* ,, Shoe ...	... per set of 3		2	0
* ,, Banister, single ...	... ... per doz.		11	0
* ,, ,, double	... ... ,,	1	1	0
* ,, Horse, body, grey, Kent's or Hamilton's	... ,,	3	6	0
* ,, Water	... ... ,,		12	0
* ,, Dandriff, millet ...	... ... ,,		12	0
* ,, Deck scrub ...	... ... ,,		15	0
* ,, Table	... ... ,,	1	1	0
* ,, Hair, Toilet, Kent's ...	... ... ,,		11	6
* ,, Nail ,, ...	... ... ,,		10	6
* ,, Black lead	... ...per set of 3		2	3
*Sash Tools, Kent's or Hamilton's—				
Nos. 1 to 3 ...	... per doz.		3	0
,, 4 to 6 ...	... ,,		6	6
,, 7 to 9 ...	... ,,		14	0
,, 10 to 12	... ,,	1	4	0

No. 13.

IRONMONGERY

Foster and Foster.

Attention is directed to the General Conditions set out in *Gazette* notice.

* Denotes that a sample is shown, but as it may be approximate it is to be read in conjunction with any fuller description given herein.

Articles.								£	s.	d.
*Adzes, Sorby's	...	...	...	...	...	...	each		3	0
Augers—½ to ⅞-inch		...	...	...	...	,,				10
* ,, 1 to 2-inch		...	...	...	...	,,			2	6
*Axes, with handles, Collins'. 4¾ to 6 lb.		...	...	...	,,				3	9
*Bath Bricks	...	...	...	...	...	per doz.			1	6
*Blacking	...	...	...	...	...	per doz. tins			1	3
Black lead	...	...	...	...	...	per lb.			0	2
Boilers, iron, 6 gallons	...	...	...	...	each			10	6
,, ,, 8 ,,	...	...	...	...	...	,,			13	3
,, ,, 10 ,,	...	...	...	...	...	,,			16	0
* ,, ,, 12 ,,	...	...	...	...	...	,,			18	0
*Braces, ratchet	...	...	...	...	...	,,			4	6
*Brace-bits	...	...	...	...	per set of 12			1	8
*Brunswick black, 10-oz. jars	...	...	...	per doz.			6	0
*Camp-ovens and covers, 22-inch		...	...	each			7	6
Charcoal	...	...	...	...	...	per bush.				5½
Chisels—Socket, ¼ to ⅞-inch	...	...	...	each				9
* ,, ,, 1 to 1½-inch	...	...	...	,,			1	9
,, Firmer, ¼ to ⅞-inch	...	...	...	,,				6
* ,, ,, 1 to 1½-inch	...	...	...	,,			1	0
*Clothes-pegs, wood	...	...	...	...	per gross				8
Cocks, brass—Fiddian—Racking, ½-inch	...	per doz.	1	1	0
* ,, ,, ,, ,, ¾-inch	...	...	,,	1	1	6
,, ,, ,, ,, ⅞-inch	...	...	,,	1	2	6
,, ,, ,, Hinged ⅞-inch, with iron-hinged					
,, ,, ,, lever, to lock	...	...	,,	1	19	0
*Corkscrews, Adelaide	...	...	...	...	...	each				6
*Curry-combs	...	...	...	...	...	per doz.			7	0
*Ears, tinned—Billycan	...	...	...	per gross of pairs		3	9
* ,, ,, Bucket	...	...	...	,,			7	3
Emery cloth	...	...	...	...	...	per quire			1	6
*Enamelled-ware—Bowls, 7¼-inch overall—10 oz.	...	per doz.		5	0
* ,, Chambers, 8¾-inch overall—19 oz.	...	each		1	3
* ,, 4¼-inch Cups and 6-inch saucers				
,, overall	...	...	...	...	per doz.			7	0
* ,, Jugs, 4-quart	...	...	...	...	each			2	6

IRONMONGERY—*continued.*

Articles.		£	s.	d.
*Enamelled-ware—Mugs, imperial pints ...	per doz.		4	6
* ,, Plates, 10-inch overall			5	0
* ,, Wash-basins, 16-inch overall—36 oz.	each		1	3
*Files—Cross-cut, 6 to 8-inch	per doz.		4	0
* ,, Hand-saw, 4 to 5½-inch	,,		2	0
* ,, Tenon-saw, 3-inch	,,		1	0
* ,, Smooth, 12-inch, round, half-round, **square**, or flat	,,		11	0
,, ,, 14-inch ,, ,, ,, ...	,,		15	0
,, ,, 16-inch ,, ,, ,,	,,		15	6
,, Second-cut, 12-inch ,, ,, ,,	,,		6	0
,, ,, 14-inch ,, ,, ,,	,,		8	0
* ,, ,, 16-inch ,, ,, ,,	,,		10	0
* ,, **Bastard** 12-inch ,, ,, ,,	,,		8	0
,, ,, 14-inch ,, ,, ,,	,,		12	6
,, ,, 16-inch ,, ,, ,,	,,		15	0
Filters—Cheavin's No. 00=½-gallon ...	each		9	0
,, ,, No. 0=2½-gallon ...	,,	1	2	0
,, ,, No. 1=3½-gallon ...	,,	1	8	0
,, ,, No. 2=5-gallon ...	,,	1	10	0
*Forks—Dinner, nickel	per doz.		5	3
* ,, Hay, 3-prong	each		1	6
* ,, Stable (Parkes'), 4-prong ...	,,		2	3
*Frypans, 14-inch overall ...	,,		1	3
Galvanised Iron—				
Corrugated, any lengths—				
Gospel Oak Anchor, 24 gauge ...	per ton	18	10	0
,, ,, 26 ,, ...	,,	19	0	0
Lysaght's Orb, 24 gauge	,,	18	10	0
,, ,, 26 ,, ...	,,	19	0	0
Plain, any sizes—				
Gospel Oak Anchor—				
22 gauge	,,	19	0	0
24 ,, ...	,,	20	10	0
26 ,, ...	,,	21	10	0
Lysaght's Queen's Head—				
22 gauge	,,	19	0	0
24 ,, ...	,,	20	10	0
26 ,, ...	,,	21	10	0
Glasses—				
* Lamp chimney—B, lip or plain	per doz.		3	0
* ,, ,, B, unbreakable, "La Bastie" ...	,,		7	6
* ,, ,, For Hinks' patent duplex burner	,,		7	0
* ,, ,, Hurricane	each			4
* ,, ,, Rochester No. 2, fire-proof, "Acme"	,,			5
Glass paper, assorted numbers	per quire			10
*Glue—Common	per lb.			8
* ,, Best Russian	,,			10
*Grease, axle, Bidwell's 2-lb. tins	,,			3
*Gridirons	each			9

IRONMONGERY—*continued.*

Articles.		Price.
		£ s. d.
Grindstones—16 to 24 ... ... per inch		2
„ 25 to 30 ... ... „		3
Grindstone mountings, Nos. 1 to 4 ... ... per set		1 3
*Hammers—Claw, Cheney's, 5 ... ... each		2 3
* „ Shoeing ... ... „		1 0
* „ Tack, magnetic ... ... „		3
*Handcuffs, assorted sizes ... ... per pair		4 0
„ Burnishing ... ... „		6
„ Re-springing ... ... „		6
„ Keys to be fitted ... ... each		6
*Handles—Axe, American No. 1 quality ... per doz.		7 6
* „ Broom ... ... „		1 8
* „ Mop ... ... „		2 6
* „ Pick ... ... „		6 6
* „ Adze ... ... „		4 0
„ Hoe, 5 ft. ... ... „		5 6
* „ Scythe, American 000 ... ... each		2 0
* „ Chest, iron 4½-inch over-all ... per gross of pairs		1 4 0
„ „ „ 3½-inch .. „ „		18 0
Hinges, T, 14 to 20 ... ... per doz. pairs		7 6
*Hoes, chipping, 0, 1, 2, ... per doz.		10 0
*Hoof-picks ... ... „		6 0
Hoop-iron, black ... . per cwt.		9 0
„ stock, 4½ x ⅛ ... ... „		9 0
*Horse-rasps, 16-inch ... ... each		1 4
Horse-shoes ... ... per cwt.		1 7 6
*Horse-clippers, Clark's No. 1 .. ... each		10 0
Iron, round, half-round, flat, or square ... per ton		9 10 0
*Irons—Leg, 3 lb. 11 oz. ... ... each		2 6
* „ Marching, 4 lb. 14 oz. ... ... „		3 6
*Iron pots, three-legged ... ... „		9
*Kettles, tea, 9 quarts ... ... „		9 6
*Knife-polish, Oakey's ... ... per doz. tins		5 0
*Knives and Forks—Dinner ... ... per doz.		9 6
* „ „ Carving ... ... per pair		2 0
*Knives—Butchers' ... ... per doz.		8 9
* „ Dinner ... ... „		5 3
* „ Shoeing ... ... „		4 0
*Ladles—Iron tinned, 5½-inch ... ... each		7
„ Britannia metal ... ... „		4
*Lamps, kerosene, with chimney and wick ... „		3 0
„ Rochester No. 2, plain nickel, complete ... „		8 6
*Lamp-burners—B ... ... per doz.		1 0
* „ Hinks' duplex, brass, with collar ...		3 0 0
*Lamp-wick, 1-inch, in rolls of 12 yards ... per roll		9
* „ in lengths of 8-in. ... doz. pieces		1½
„ for Rochester No. 2 ... per doz.		1 0
*Lanterns—Bull's-eye, Dolan's patent crescent ... „		4 16 0
* „ Hurricane ... ... each		3 6
Lead, pig ... ... per lb.		1¾
Lime ... ... per bag of 2 cwt.		4 9

IRONMONGERY—*continued.*

Articles.		Price. £ s. d.
*Locks—Box, brass lever, 3-inch, with screws	each	6
,, ,, ,, 4-inch ,,	,,	8
* ,, Pad, brass, Chubb. 2-inch	,,	14 0
,, ,, ,, ,, 2½-inch	,,	16 0
* ,, ,, ,, ,, 3-inch	,,	17 0
* ,, ,, galvanised iron, 2½-inch	,,	6
Matches—		
Bryant and May or Bell and Black—Wax—		
250's	per gross of boxes	12 0
1000's	,,	2 8 0
Nails—Wire, sorts as required, 1-inch to 6-inch	per cwt.	15 0
,, Horseshoe, globe, assorted	per lb.	5
,, Clout, 1-inch to 2-inch	per cwt.	10 0
,, Copper, boat, with rooves	per lb.	11
* ,, Moulded lead-headed, any size or gauge	,,	2
*Needles, packing	per doz.	3
*Oilstones—Turkey	per lb.	1 0
* ,, in cedar cases	per doz.	1 2 6
Pencils, carpenters, Rowney's best	,,	9
*Planes—Jack, Mathieson's	each	4 9
* ,, Smoothing, Mathieson's	,,	4 0
*Picks, with handles	,,	3 3
Pumice-stone, large lumps	per lb.	3
Rakes, iron—14-tooth	each	6
* ,, 18-tooth	,,	1 3
*Razors, Bengal, ⅜-inch	,,	3 0
*Reaping-hooks, No. 4		9
Rivets and washers, galvanised iron tank	per cwt.	1 8 0
,, ,, copper, sizes as required. 1-lb. pkts.	per lb.	1 0
Rivets—Tinman's Nos. 6 to 9	per 1,000	4
,, ,, Nos. 10 to 12	,,	1 0
,, ,, Nos. 13 to 15	,,	1 4
*Rules, 2-foot, fourfold	each	9
Saucepans—2 quarts	,,	2 0
,, 3 ,,	,,	2 4
* ,, 4 ,,	,,	2 9
,, 6 ,,	,,	3 8
*Saws—Hand, 26-inch, Diston's	,,	4 9
* ,, Crosscut, 6-ft. ,,	,,	7 3
,, Tenon, 12 in. ,,	,,	2 6
*Sawsets—Hand	,,	4
* ,, Crosscut	,,	8
*Scales, counter (Avery's), No. 3	,,	18 0
,, ,, ,, No. 4	,,	1 2 0
*Scissors—Barbers', 8-inch, Seymour's	per pair	2 6
* ,, Tailors', 8-inch, Johnson's	,,	1 9
Screws—Wood. ⅓-inch to 1-inch	per gross	5
,, ,, 1½-inch to 2-inch	,,	9
,, ,, 2⅜-inch to 3-inch	,,	1 0
,, Brass. ½ ,, 1 ,,	,,	1 7
,, ,, 1⅛ ,, 2 ,,	,,	3 9

Articles.		Price.
		£ s. d.
*Screwdrivers—Steel, 4 to 7-inch ... ... each		5
„ „ 8 to 12-inch ... ... „		9
*Scythe blades ... ... „		2 8
* „ stones ... ... per doz.		2 8
„ boards ... ... each		4
Shades, lamp, Rochester, No. 2 ... ... „		1 0
*Shovels—Long ... ... „		2 1
* „ Short ... ... „		2 1
* „ Firing, steel, No. 7, 12-inch ... ... „		2 6
Solder ... ... per lb.		10
*Soldering Irons, No. 7 ... ... each		2 6
*Spades, Parkes' ... ... „		3 0
*Spoons—Table, tinned iron ... ... per doz.		1 9
* „ solid nickel ... ... „		5 3
„ Tea „ ... ... „		1 0
*Steels, butchers' ... ... each		1 6
*Strops, razor, Canton, Cowran ... ... „		4 6
Tacks—Blued, cut, ¼-inch to 1-inch ... ... per 1,000		2
„ Tinned „ „ ... ... „		2½
„ Copper, any size ... ... per lb.		9
*Tapes, measuring, Chesterman's metallic, 66-ft. ... each		6 6
Tin—Ingot ... ... per cwt 6	1	4
„ Plate, 1x charcoal, 20 in. x 14 in. ... ... per box. 0	18	0
„ „ 2x „ „ „ ... ... „	1 1	0
„ „ 3x „ „ „ ... ... „	2 2	0
„ „ 1x „ „ 16 in. ... ... „	0 18	0
„ „ 1c „ „ 14 in. ... ... „	0 15	0
„ „ 24 gauge, 72 x 30 inch ... ... per plate 0	4	0
*Tomahawks, American, Collins' ... ... per doz. 1	7	0
*Trapscrews, 2½-inch ... ... „	1 1	0
Washboards, wood ... ... each	0 0	7½
*Weights, scale—4 lb. down to ½-oz. (9 pieces) ... per set	0 1	0
* „ „ 7lb. and 14 lb. ... ... at per lb.	0 0	1
„ brass, for letter balances, 8-oz. to ¼-oz.		
(6 pieces) ... ... per set.	0 0	9
*Wheelbarrows—Galvanised, small ... ... each	1 5	0
„ „ large ... ... „	1 6	6
*Whistles ... ... per doz.	0 3	0
Wire, Tinman's hard—Nos. 4 to 10 ... ... per bundle		
	of ½-cwt. 0	6	6
„ „ „ Nos. 11 to 16 ... ... „	0 7	0
Zinc, perforated ... ... per sheet 0	2	0

———

IRONMONGERY—*continued.*

Ammunition—Martini-Henri carbine and rifle.
      ,,   Revolver, Webley, ·442.
      ,,   Snider, Carbine or Rifle.
Basins, tin, wash-hand.
Bedsteads, iron, stump, folding.
Billys, round, 1 to 8 quarts.
  ,, half-round, in nests of five.
Boxes, G.I., for earth.
Buckets, G.I.
    ,,   slop.
    ,,   tea.
    ,,   milk.
Candlesticks, japanned.
Cans, water, 12 qts.
  ,, watering, galvanized iron (large) and tin (small).
  . meat.
  ,, soup.
  ,, tea with taps.
  ,, tea with spouts.
  ,, vegetable.
Cash-boxes.
Chambers, tin.
Dippers, tin, $2\frac{1}{4}$ and 4 quarts.
Dishes, tin, oval, 16" x 13" and 13" x 10".
  ,, baking, about 20" x 15" x $2\frac{1}{2}$".
  ,, wash-up, about 23" x 19" x $6\frac{3}{4}$".
Handles, Turk's head, long or telescopic.
Jackshays.
Kerosine.
Lamps, Rochester.
  ,, tin, with burners, large and small.
Lanterns, stable.
Lids for E.C. pans, round, 12 in. and 14 in. diameter.
Matches, Safety.
Mats, coir, from 27" to 48" wide x 16" to 30" deep.
  ,, ,, wool bordered, 1' 0" x 2' 8" or.
Pans, E.C., round, 14" x 16" and 14" x 12".
  ,, dust.
Plates, tin.
Pots, tea, 3 and 5 quarts.
  ,, half-pint, pint, and quart.
Scoops, tin.
Tanks, G.I., 600, 800, and 1,000 gallons.
Tubs, cell, airtight.
  ,, washing.

No. 14.

CANVAS, CORD, ETC.

G. H. Adams and Co.

Attention is directed to the General Conditions set out in *Gazette* notice.

* Denotes that a sample is shown, but as it may be approximate it is to be read in conjunction with any fuller description given herein.

The actual net weight only of cord will be paid for.

Articles.							Price.		
							£	s.	d.
*Canvas—24-inch Navy, No. 1 ...			...	...	...	per yard			7
,,	,,	,, No. 2 ...	...			,,			6½
,,	,,	,, No. 3 ...	...	...	...	,,			6
,,	,,	,, No. 4 ...	...	...	...	,,			5½
,,	,,	,, No. 5 ...	...	...	...	,,			5
* ,,	,,	Long Flax, No. 1		...	...	,,			10¾
,,	,,	,, No. 2		...	...	,,			10¼
,,	,,	,, No. 3 ...	...	...	...	,,			9¾
,,	,,	,, No. 4 ...	...	...	...	,,			9½
* ,,	36-inch Long Flax, No. 1	...	...	...	,,		1		3¾
*Cotton Waste	...	...	...	...	...	... per lb.			3½
*Cord—Strong, 16-oz., 6 ply, 90 lb. strain on 9 ft.			... per doz. lb.				7		6
* ,,	Medium, 8-oz., 4 ,, 60 lb.	,,	,,		,,		7		3
* ,,	Fine, 4-oz., 3 ,, 15 lb.	,,	,,	...	,,		11		9
*Twine—Roping, 5 ply ...		...	...	...	... per lb.				10½
* ,,	Seaming, 3 ply ...	...	...	...	...	,,			10½

No. 15.

SADDLERS' IRONMONGERY.

Butler Bros.

Attention is directed to the General Conditions set out in *Gazette* notice.

* Denotes that a sample is shown, but as it may be approximate it is to be read in conjunction with any fuller description given herein.

	Articles.		Price. £	s.	d.
	Awls, bayonet	per gross		8	6
	Awl-hafts, assorted	per doz.		1	6
*	Burnishers, chain	"		18	0
*	Bells, horse, with straps	each		1	9
	Buckles—Brass roller, ½-inch	per gross		5	0
	" " " ⅝ "	"		6	0
*	" " " ¾ "	"		7	0
	" " " ⅞ "	"		8	0
	" " " 1 "	"		10	0
*	" " " 1¼ "	"		12	0
*	" " belt, 2½ "	"	2	2	0
	" Tinned roller, ¾ "	"		1	9
*	" " " 1 "	"		3	3
	" " " 1¼ "	"		4	0
*	" Nickel-plated dees, ½-inch	"		3	6
	" " " ⅝ "	"		3	9
	" " " ¾ "	"		4	0
	" " " ⅞ "	"		4	3
	" " " 1 "	"		4	6
*	" Stirrup-leather, 1¼ "	"		6	0
	" Nickel-plated whole, ½-inch ...	"		4	0
	" " " ⅝ " ...	"		4	9
*	" " " ¾ " ...	"		5	6
	" " " ⅞ " ...	"		6	3
	" " " 1 " ...	"		7	0
	" " half-square, ½ inch ...	"		3	6
	" " " ⅝ " ...	"		3	9
	" " " ¾ " ...	"		4	0
*	" " " ⅞ " ...	"		4	3
	" " " 1 " ...	"		4	6
	" Hobble, Japanned, 1⅜-inch	"		9	6
*	" " " 1½ "	"		10	0
*	" Girth, bar loop	"		6	6
	" Japanned, gear, 1-inch	"		4	0
	" " " 1¼ "	"		4	3
	" " " 1½ "	"		5	0
*	" " " 1¾ "	"		6	0

SADDLERS' IRONMONGERY—*continued.*

Articles.		Prices. £	s.	d.
Buckles, Japanned, gear, 2-inch	per gross		7	6
" " " 3 "	"		13	0
Back chains, to average 7 lb. each	per lb.			3
*Bits—Weymouth, hard steel, with bridoons	each		6	6
* " Snaffle, steel	per doz.	1	16	0
Breeching chains	per pair		1	4
*Coachaline, 1 lb. tins	per doz.		10	0
*Comb, mane—horn, 5-inch	"		5	6
Dees—Brass, ⅝-inch	per gross		3	0
" " ¾ "	"		3	0
" " ⅞ "	"		3	6
" " 1 "	"		4	0
" Japanned, 2-inch	"		6	0
" Nickel-plated, ½-inch	"		3	6
* " " ¾ "	"		3	9
" " ⅞ "	"		4	0
" " 1 "	"		4	6
" Tinned ⅞ "	"		1	3
Dye, Harris's black harness	per bottle			7
*Hair—Doe	per cwt.	1	5	8
* " Horse, curled	per lb.		1	9
*Hames—Leading, full-cased steel	per pair		3	9
* " Shaft " "	"		4	0
*Hemp—Barbour's best Irish Flax, No. 15, white	per 1½ lb. paper of 24 balls		5	3
" " " " yellow			5	6
* " " Common Scotch, white, per 3 lb. paper of 24 balls			8	0
*Hobble chains, 16 oz.	per gross	1	19	0
*Hogskins—English, not less than 4 feet x 4 feet 6 inches clear of shoulders and bellies	each	1	12	6
*Horse scrapers	"		2	0
Leather—Black patent middling, not less than 2 x 4 feet, free of shoulders and bellies ...	per side	1	1	0
* " Best English Oak-tanned Bridle, light stained, in butts, containing about 10 square feet and about 5 lb. in weight	per lb.		3	9
*Manger Chains, about 26 oz.	each		1	3
Needles—Harness, any size	per paper			3
" Saddlers' sewing	"			3
*Nails—Saddlers' clout, any size	per lb.			11
* " " plated, 1¼ inch	per gross		3	3
* " Brass, ¾-inch	"		1	6
*Punches—1 to 6	each			5
" 7 " 10	"			8
" 11 " 15	"		1	0
Rings—Brass, 1-inch	per gross		12	0
" " 1¼ "	"		14	0
* " " 1½ "	"		18	0
" " 1¾ "	"	1	4	0

SADDLERS' IRONMONGERY—*continued.*

Articles.		Price. £	s.	d.
Rings—Japanned, 1¼-inch	per gross		3	9
,, ,, 1½ ,, ...	,,		4	0
* ,, ,, 1¾ ,, ...	,,		4	3
,, ,, 2 ,, ...	,,		5	0
,, Nickel-plated, 1-inch	,,		6	6
* ,, ,, 1¼ ,, ...	,,		9	0
,, ,, 1½ ,, ...	,,		10	0
,, ,, 1¾ ,, ...	,,		12	0
,, Tinned, 1-inch	,,		2	6
,, ,, 1⅛ ,, ...	,,		2	6
* ,, ,, 1¼ ,, ...	,,		3	3
* ,, ,, 1½ ,, ...	,,		4	0
,, ,, 1¾ ,, ...	,,		6	0
*Saddle cloths, blue, seamless and strapped ...	each		6	6
*Saddle-trees—Pack, beech	,,		3	9
* ,, Riding, *steel-plated*, C. H. May's, any size	,,		10	0
*Snake hooks and buckles, brass, 1½-inch	per set of 4 pieces			3
,, ,, ,, 1¾ ,,	,, ,,			4
,, ,, ,, 2 ,,	,, ,,			5
*Spring hooks—steel, 1-inch	per gross	2	5	0
* ,, brass ,, ...	,,	2	14	0
*Spurs—Solid nickel, rowel half-covered ...	per pair		2	0
* ,, Military, solid nickel	,,		4	0
*Staples, saddle, plated	per gross		9	0
*Stirrup-irons, solid nickel	per pair		4	0
Studs—Brass, cone top, ⅜ shank, ⅝ over all ...	per gross		9	6
,, ,, ,, ⅝ ,, ¾ ,, ...	,,		9	6
* ,, Plated	,,		11	0
*Twine, quilting	per ball		1	3
*Tacks, saddlers', ¼ to 1-inch, Crown brand	per 1,000			4
*Trace chains, leading, 20 lb. per pair, bright ...	per lb.			3
*Wash leathers, chamoised, not less than 26 x 24 ...	per doz.	1	0	0
*Web—Straining	per piece		7	3
,, White race wool, 2-inch	,,		6	9
*Whips, cart, 36-inch, with kangaroo thong ...	each		3	9

SADDLERS' IRONMONGERY—*continued.*

The following lines of Saddlery, &c., are in Stock at the Government Stores :—

Bandoliers (shoulder and belt).
Belts—Revolver, cartridge.
   ,,   Waist, for men and boys.
Breastplates, Police.
Bridles, bush.
Buckets, gun.
Cloths, saddle, Police.
Cruppers.
Girths, saddle.
Halters, hemp.
Headstalls, leather.
Hobbles, with straps.
Pack bags—
    Leather, large
    Canvas, large and small.
Pouches—
    Handcuff.
    Revolver.
    Saddle.
    Tomahawk.
Rugs, horse.
Saddles, town Police.
   ,,   bush.
   ,,   pack.
Slings, revolver pouch.
Stirrup leathers.
Straps—Dee, hame, hobble, pack side, saddle, and spur.
Surcingles, riding and pack.
Tents, with flys : 6 x 9, 8 x 10, 10 x 12.
Valises, roll, saddle, 34" x 4"
Water-bags, canvas.

No. 16.

L E A T H E R.

M. J. Gallagher.

Attention is directed to the General Conditions set out in *Gazette* notice.

* Denotes that a sample is shown, but as it may be approximate it is to be read in conjunction with any fuller description given herein.

The price of 1 lb. will be deducted for every brand on leathers scheduled at per lb. Leathers scheduled at per side must be absolutely free of brands.

Brown harness to weigh 16 lb. per side for leather measuring 40 inches by a line drawn from back to belly across the centre of side, and not to exceed 1 inch on the same line for every lb. over 16 ; sides below 16 lb. to measure proportionately less by a similar line.

Bridle to be clean both sides, and to weigh a lb. for every foot of length from neck to butt.

Articles.		Price. £ s. d.
*Leather—Sole, 22 lb. ...	per lb.	11
* „ „ 18 „	„	9¾
* „ Kip, not exceeding 9 lb.	„	1 1¾
* „ Tweed „ 7 „	„	1 6½
* „ Brown Harness—(*see special note*)	„	1 0½
* „ Black „ 17 to 22 lb. ...	„	1 2½
* „ Bag, 7 to 8 lb.	per side	14 0
* „ „ black, fast colour ..	„	15 0
* „ Saddle flap, 15 to 18 lb.	„	17 0
* „ Bridle { See special note }	„	14 0
* „ „ stained to colour of sample { }	„	15 0
Basils—Saddlers', 12 lb. to the doz.	per doz.	14 6
„ Shoemakers', 9 lb. to the doz. ... ... „		11 0

No. 17.

GRINDERY.

John Hunter.

Attention is directed to the General Conditions set out in *Gazette* notice.

* Denotes that a sample is shown, but as it may be approximate it is to be read in conjunction with any fuller description given herein.

Articles.		Price.		
		£	s.	d.
*Awls—Peg, ⅝-in., round or square	per gross		2	8
* ,, Sewing	,,		4	10
* ,, Stabbing	,,		5	4
* ,, Hafts, Sewing	per doz.		1	2
* ,, ,, Pegging	,,		8	10
*Boots, women's goloshed E.S. lasting, sizes... ...	,,	3	3	0
Bottom Balls				4
*Eyelets, brass, No. 08 or 09	per 1,000			6
Ink, burnishing	per quart bottle			7
*Knives, hand	per doz.		5	10
Lasts—Iron—Men's, youths', and women's, assorted	per lb.			4
,, Wood ,, ,, ,,	per pair		1	10
°Measures, tape, 2 feet	per doz.		3	0
*Nails—1-inch, fla-top wire	per lb.			3
* ,, Tip	,,			3
* ,, Hungarian	,,			3
*Pegs, shoe, wood, assorted	,,			3½
Rasps—7-inch	per doz.		7	0
,, 10-inch	,,		10	0
* ,, 12-inch	,,		14	6
* ,, Peg	,,		17	6
*Rivets, brass, any size	per lb.		1	0
*Sprigs, assorted	,,			2
*Tacks—Lasting, assorted	per gross		1	0
* ,, Tingles, assorted	per lb.			4½
*Thread, yellow, machine, three or six cord, any number	,,		12	6
*Tips, heel, assorted	per gross		17	6

No. 18.

SHIP CHANDLERY.

Perry Brothers.

Attention is directed to the General Conditions set out in *Gazette* notice.

* Denotes that a sample is shown, but as it may be approximate it is to be read in conjunction with any fuller description given herein.

Articles.		Price.
		£ s. d.
Beeswax	per lb.	10
*Blue lights, signal	per doz.	18 0
Boat hooks—Heads only, galvanised iron	each	1 0
„ „ Staves	„	9
Chain, galvanised, 7/16 to ½ inch, with certificate ...	per cwt.	1 10 0
Coir fibre	„	10 0
Cork fenders, best coir	„	1 8 0
Lamp cotton	per lb.	10
Lime lights, Holmes's	per doz.	12 0
*Needles, seaming, any number	„	1 0
Oars, ash	per foot	6
Oils—Sweet	per gal.	4 6
„ Castor	„	2 8
„ Tea	„	3 9
„ Colza	„	3 9
* „ Castorine	„	2 6
„ Neatsfoot	„	2 3
„ Rangoon	„	3 0
„ Cylinder, Crane's	„	3 0
Packing—Flax	per lb.	9
* „ Paragon, ⅝ to 1 inch	„	2 0
* „ Tuck's patent, ¾ to 1½	„	1 6
„ Asbestos sheet, ⅛ and ¼	„	6
*Palms, sewing, Squire's	per doz.	12 0
Pitch, Swedish, in lb. boxes	per lb.	2
Resin	„	1
*Rockets, with sticks	per doz.	1 8 0
Rope—Coir	per cwt.	2 0 0
„ Europe	„	2 14 0
„ Hambro line	per lb.	6
„ Ratline	per cwt.	2 16 0
„ Marline	per lb.	8
„ Spunyarn	„	6
* „ White line	„	9
„ Manilla, white, ¼-inch upwards	per cwt.	2 16 0
* „ Signal halyards, any size	per lb.	1 0

SHIP CHANDLERY—*continued.*

Articles.							Price.		
							£	s.	d.
Rowlocks, brass ...	...	...	...	...	...	per lb.		2	6
,, galvanised iron		...	...	...	...	per pair		2	0
*Scrapers, ship	...	...	...	...	...	each		1	0
Seizing wire	...	...	...	...	...	per lb.			6
Soft soap, in tins of any required size				...	...	per cwt.	1	5	0
Soap lees ... · ...	...	...	...	...	...	per gal.		1	3
*Sponge cloths	...	...	...	...	...	per doz.		1	6
Squeegees, as per description	...	...	...	...	each		4	0
Tallow	...	...	...	...	...	per cwt.	1	1	0
Tar—Coal	...	...	...	...	...	per gal.			4
,, Stockholm ...	...	...	...	...	...	,,		1	6
*Zinc plates (rolled), 12 x 6 x ¾		...	...	...	per cwt.	1	10	0

In stock also at Government Stores :—

Oakum in 50 lb. dholls.

No. 19.

PAINTS, OILS, ETC.

Thomas Brown and Sons, Limited.

Attention is directed to the General Conditions set out in *Gazette* notice.
Glass trade list to be attached to tender.

Articles.		Price. £	s.	d.
Dryers, patent ... ... per cwt.			17	6
Iron, Oxide of, in oil ... ... ,,			18	6
Oil—Linseed, raw, Blundell, Spence, and Co. ... per gal.			3	6
„ „ boiled, „ ... ,,			3	8
Paint—White lead, Champion's genuine ... ... per cwt.	1	10	6
„ „ Hubbuck's „ ... ... ,,	1	9	0
„ „ Storer's „ ... ... ,,	1	8	6
„ White zinc, Hubbuck's ... ... ,,	1	7	6
„ Red lead... ... ... ,,	1	2	0
„ Red lead, in oil... ... ... ,,		18	0
„ Red oxide ... ... ,,		18	6
„ Black, in oil ... ... ,,		18	0
„ Vegetable-black ... ... per lb.			5
„ Dark-green, in oil ... ... per cwt.		19	6
„ Yellow ochre ... ... ,,		12	0
„ Yellow ochre, in oil ... ... ,,		17	0
„ Carter's Anti-fouling ... ... ,,	1	10	0
„ Mixed, ready for use, any colour ... per lb.			4
„ Pacific Rubber Co., any colour ... per gal.		7	6
Turpentine ... ... ,,		3	4½
Varnish—Black Japan ... ... ,,		9	0
„ Copal ... ... ,,		9	6
„ Carriage ... ... ,,		12	0
„ Gold size ... ... ,,		8	3
Whiting ... ... per cwt.		3	6
Glass, sheet, at per cent. discount off attached List prices		20 %		

The following are also in Stock at Government Stores :—

Oil, Salad, 12 oz. bottles.
„ Machine, 2 or 3 oz. bottles.

No. 20.

FLAGS.

George Smith.

Attention is directed to the General Conditions set out in *Gazette* notice.

Flags to be *hand-sewn with worsted throughout*, and toggled.

Bunting to be of the quality of the standard samples ; blue must stand the test for true indigo dye.

Every flag to have the number of the order worked into the border nearest the taff.

Articles.		Price.
		£ s. d.
Ensigns, with jack, any size, including the insertion of required badge, which will be supplied to the Contractor ... ... per sq. yard		4 0
Union Jacks, any size ... ... „		4 1

The following are kept in Stock at Government Stores :—

Badge of the Colony, 10″, 13″, and 16″.

Customs Crowns, 6″, 9″, and 12″.

No. 21.

MEDICINES, CHEMICALS, ETC.

Elliott Brothers, Limited.

Attention is directed to the General conditions set out in *Gazette* notice.
* Denotes that a standard sample is kept at Government Stores.
No charge to be made for bottles or packages.
If required, goods to be securely packed for long transit free of charge.
All medicines to be fully labelled.
Prescriptions, where named, may be seen at Government Stores.
The measures named are all imperial.

Articles.		Price.		
		£	s.	d.
Acid—Carbolic, pure, crystals ... ... per lb.			1	4
„ „ crude ... ... per gal.			2	0
„ Muriatic ... ... „			2	3
„ Tartaric ... ... per lb.			1	2
„ Oxalic ... ... „				5
„ Boracic ... ... „				4
Alum—Lump ... ... „				1½
„ Powder ... ... „				1¼
Ammonia, strong solution ... ... per pint				5
Aniseed, Powell's Balsam of ... ... per doz. 1s. 1½d. bots.			12	6
Arnica, tincture of ... ... per pint			2	3
Arsenic ... ... per lb.				3
Black draught ... ... per pint				6
Bluestone (sulphate of copper) ... ... per lb.				2½
Borax—Crystals ... ... „				2¼
„ Powder ... ... „				2¼
Calomel (subchloride of mercury) ... ... per oz.				3½
Camphor—Tablets, 1 oz. in lb. tin boxes ... ... per lb.			2	1
„ Lump ... ... „			2	0
Carbolic Powder—Calvert's, original 1-lb. dredgers per doz.			8	6
„ Quibell's, „ „			8	9
„ Calvert's, „ 2-lb. „ „			13	0
„ Quibell's, „ „ „			11	9
„ Calvert's, not less than 15% carbolic per cwt.			14	0
„ Quibell's, „ „ „			17	0
Chloride of lime ... ... per lb.				2
Chlorodyne, Collis Browne's ... ... per doz. 1s. 1½d. bots.			11	10
Chloroform, Duncan and Flockhart, best white label per lb.			7	4
Condy's Powder ... ... per doz. 1-lb. tins			10	0
„ Fluid ... ... per doz. pints		1	5	6
Copperas (sulphate of iron) ... ... per lb.				1
Cough mixture (prescription), 8-oz. bottles ... ... per doz.			6	0
Cream of tartar ... ... per lb.				10½

MEDICINES, CHEMICALS, Etc.—*continued.*

Articles.		Price. £ s. d.
Diarrhœa mixture (prescription), 8-oz. bottles	... per doz.	5 0
Disinfecting fluid, Little's	... per gallon	6 0
„ „ Quibell's	... „	6 3
Dover's powder	... per oz.	2½
Embrocation—Elliman's 2s. 6d. bottles ...	...per doz. bots. 1	5 0
„ Farmer's Friend, Rowe's ...	... „ 1	8 0
Epsom salts, in oz. pkts.	... per lb.	1¾
Eye lotion (prescription), 8-oz. bottles ...	... per doz.	2 6
Fever and ague mixture (prescription), 8-oz. bottles...	„	4 6
Flour of sulphur	... per lb.	1½
Friar's balsam	... per pint	2 6
Fuller's earth	... per lb.	1¼
Glycerine, Price's genuine, labelled ...	„	2 1
Ink, marking, 1s. bottles	... per bottle	6
Insectibane, Rocke's	per doz 1s. tins	6 2
Insecticide, Kruse's	„	6 0
Iodine	... per oz.	1 2
„ Tincture of, in 1-lb. bottles ...	... per lb.	2 8
Iodoform	... per oz.	1 3
Ipecacuanha wine	per pint	1 6
Iron, tincture of	... per lb.	8
Laudanum (tincture of opium)... ...	... per pint	2 6
Liniment, soap	... per pint	1 10
Linseed meal	... per lb.	1½
Liquorice, Solazzi	„	1 9
Magnesia, carbonate of	„	6
„ Fluid, Kruse's	per doz. 1s. bots.	7 10
Nitre, sweet (spirits of ether)	... per pint	2 4
Oil—Castor	„	5
„ Carbolic	„	6
„ Cod Liver	„	10
„ Eucalyptus	„	1 3
„ of Turpentine, rectified	„	5
„ St. Jacobs	...per doz. bots. 1	5 0
Ointment—Australian, Josephson's ...	„ small pots	9 10
„ Holloway's	„ 1s. 1½d. pots	12 6
„ Blistering, Stevens' ...	„ small tins 1	8 0
„ „ James' ...	„ small pots	16 0
„ Zinc	... per lb.	9
„ Mercurial	„	2 7
„ Basilicon	„	7
Opium—Lump	... per oz.	2 8
„ Powder...	„	2 8
Painkiller (Perry Davis's)	per doz. bots.	11 3
Pearlash	per cwt. 1	6 0
Pills—Aperient (prescription)	in bots. of 1 gross	1 3
„ Podophyllin, in bottles of 1 gross	per gross	1 9
„ Cockle's	per doz 1s. 1½d. boxes	12 3
„ Beecham's	„ „	12 3
„ Holloway's	„ „	12 8
„ Warner's	per doz. boxes	9 6

MEDICINES, CHEMICALS, Etc.—*continued.*

Articles.		Price.		
		£	s.	d.
Quinine, Howard's	per oz.		1	9
Sal-ammoniac (chloride of ammonia)...	per lb.			6¼
Saltpetre (nitrate of potash)	,,			3¼
Senna	,,			6
Soap—Pear's Toilet, 4-oz. tablets	per 3-lb. box		3	4
„ Calvert's 10 °/₀ Carbolic, 3 tablets in box	per box		1	2
Soda—Caustic	per lb.			3¼
„ Carbonate of	,,			1¼
Strychnine	per oz.		2	5
*Sponge—Honeycomb (free from sand)	,,		1	3
* „ Turkey „ „	,,		2	0
Sulphur Roll	per cwt.		9	0
Tapers—Wax, 12 inches	per box			10
„ „ 18 to 22 inches	per lb.		1	6
Tartar emetic (antimony)	per oz.			1½
Vaseline, Cheeseborough's, 1-lb. tins ...	per lb.		1	2
Warner's Safe Cure	per doz. 5s. bots. 2	5	0	
Zinc—Oxide of	per lb.			6
„ Sulphate of	,,			4
„ Muriate of, liquid	,,			6

The following are also obtainable from the Government Stores :—

Alabastrine or Moth Marbles.
Candles, Apollo, 16 oz.
Gum-Arabic, picked Turkey White.
Monkey Soap.
Soda Crystals.
Soap, Washing No. 1, 44-bar.

No. 22.

TIMBER.

Dath, Henderson, Bartholomew, and Co., Limited.

Attention is directed to General Conditions set out in *Gazette* notice.
The timber must be of the best quality, and without sap.

Articles.		Price. £ s. d.
Cedar, all sizes up to 12 in. x 1 in. ... ... per foot		4½
Pine—Scantling, all sizes up to 12 in. x 12 in. per 100 sup. ft.		14 0
„ Boards, 12 in. x 1 in. ,,		14 0
,, „ 16 in. x 1 in. ... ·,		14 0
„ „ 20 in. x 1 in. ... ... ,,		14 0
(or any less thickness or width if required)		
„ Dressed Boards—Flooring, lining, partition, chamfered, and shelving, any usual trade size ... ... ,,		16 0
Hardwood—Rough, scantling, all sizes up to 12 in. x 12 in. ... ... ,,		13 6
„ „ boards, all sizes up to 12 in. x 1 in. „		13 6
„ Dressed boards, flooring and chamfered, usual trade sizes ... ... ,,		16 0
„ Arris rails out of 4 in. x 4 in.... per 100 lin. ft.		10 0
,, „ „ 5 in. x 5 in. ... ... „		16 0
Beech, rough, all sizes up to 12 in. x 12 in. ... per 100 sup. ft.		18 0

By Authority: Edmund Gregory, Government Printer, William street, Brisbane.

www.ingramcontent.com/pod-product-compliance
Lightning Source LLC
Chambersburg PA
CBHW032123080426
42733CB00008B/1039